Sara'
Secret Cipher

Written by Nadine Cowan
Illustrated by Nadine Cowan and Moka Celess

Collins

Chapter 1

The smell of curried goat wafted from the kitchen like a warm hug, and the sound of reggae music mingled with the clang of metal spoons as customers shared food and gossip at Blue Mahoes.

Aniyah and her cousin EJ's family restaurant served the best Caribbean food in London.

Aniyah, EJ and Aniyah's best friend Olivia were helping with the lunch-time rush.

Aniyah took the money, while EJ and Olivia handed Errol, a regular customer, a paper bag of warm saltfish fritters, a callaloo patty and a bowl of red pea soup.

"Thanks for your help," said Aniyah's mum. "Go and play now."

"Are you sure? I like helping," said EJ, shoving fried plantain into his mouth.

"You like eating, that's for sure!" Errol boomed.

Aniyah's mum laughed. "It's more important for you to play and be in school."

EJ raced downstairs to the basement. "Let's play Ludi!"

By the time Aniyah and Olivia entered the basement, EJ was already setting up the old wooden board game.

There was something extraordinary about the Ludi board. Etched on the side were the words:

Roll double six, or double three,
let's learn about your history.

Every time they played, something magical happened.

"I can't wait until I'm a grown-up," said EJ. "I'll go to work and make billions. I'll buy lots of racing cars and sweets and dominate the world!"

"I'm going to be a sensational skating superstar and I'll live in a mansion filled with Pomeranian puppies," gushed Olivia.

Aniyah threw the dice. They skipped across the board and landed on double three. They all grinned as a magical puff of iridescent smoke billowed out from the board, turning into a tornado that formed a wormhole and pulled them in.

Chapter 2

Aniyah was in the middle of a crowd of people emerging from the cramped and weathered buildings that lined the cobblestone roads: men, women and children, their faces etched with tiredness as they jostled forward in unison, like a school of fish.

Aniyah couldn't see Olivia or EJ.

Aniyah glanced down at her tattered apron. *Where has the game transported us to this time?* she wondered. *Maybe the women chatting will give me a clue.*

"Morning, Susan," one of the women said.

"Morning, Barbara. It's been a mither for all of us with Colin still poorly. Doctor says it's his lungs. But we do what we must to make ends meet," explained Susan, as she fastened her shawl.

"Aye," Barbara nodded glumly.

They don't sound like Londoners, Aniyah thought.

A bell rang, making Aniyah jump. Then two familiar faces appeared in the crowd.

"Olivia! EJ!" Aniyah shouted. They were looking down at a piece of paper.

"*There* you are!" said EJ.

"What's that?" asked Aniyah.

"EJ arrived with a map," Olivia replied.

"I don't recognise the street names," said EJ. He folded up the map and put it in his pocket. "We'll work it out later."

Aniyah and Olivia linked arms as they continued to march. Their worn-out shoes offered no protection from the cobbles.

They looked towards the dark silhouettes dominating the skyline. Smoke billowed from tall chimneys.

As they got closer, Aniyah looked up at the giant sooty red-brick-and-iron structure towering over them. There was a large sign on the building: Ancoat's Cotton & Co.

"I don't like it in here," Olivia whispered, as they stepped through the gates.

"Let's just follow everyone else," EJ suggested. "We'll soon find out where and when we are."

A stifling heat hit them; a musty humid odour blended with the smell of hot oil wafted up their noses. They could hear gears churning, and a rhythmic clattering sound.

Rows of looms stood like soldiers, operated by workers with nimble hands.

"Those machines are so loud!" said Aniyah.

"Look! A calendar." EJ took a closer look.

"It says 1859!" gasped Aniyah.

"Aye, it be nice if you could get to work before 1860," yelled an angry voice.

A large man headed towards them. "Get to the weavers before I dock your wages and you'll have nowt!"

"Weavers?" asked Olivia.

Aniyah gulped. "You want us to work here?"

"The yarn isn't going to weave itself!" replied the man. "You must be new. I'm Mr Elliot – the foreman. Follow me and be quick about it!"

EJ grinned at the others. "We're going to have real jobs!"

Chapter 3

They scurried past rows of looms. Workers illuminated by gas lamps transformed thread into fabric, strand by strand.

Dust and lint waltzed in the cast of the sun's rays, attempting to shine through the murky windows, before settling on the floor.

Clatter, rattle, bang! went the spinning machines as their levers thrust and whirred.

"You'll work here as a piecer," said Mr Elliot, pointing to Olivia. "You, girl! Show this one what to do."

The young girl turned to Olivia. "I'm Ada. Let's get started. Mr Elliot doesn't take kindly to idleness."

"What does a piecer do?" asked Olivia, looking at the spinning wheel.

"We repair broken threads on the machines by tying them together," Ada told her. "You work on the top end, and I'll mend from the bottom."

It was Aniyah's turn next.

"Let me see. You, girl. I have another bobbin doffer. Quickly show her what to do and get back to work, else I'll dock your wages!" snarled Mr Elliot.

The girl smiled shyly. "I'm Annie. You'll be replacing the full bobbins with empty ones so that the looms can keep going. This is a doffer hook and you use it like this."

Mr Elliot turned to EJ. "I've got just the job for you." He pointed to a small boy nearby. "You, lad! Show this boy what to do."

"My name's EJ ..."

But Mr Elliot was already walking away.

"Don't bother, he'll never use it. You from London, running away from The Great Stink?" chuckled the boy.

EJ pulled a face. "Something like that." He'd learnt about the Great Stink at school. The Victorians used to dump all their waste into the Thames. The stink coming off the river was awful.

"I'm Thomas, but we might as well all be the same person to Mr Elliot."

"He's mean," EJ said.

"We'd better get to work before you find out just how mean he can be!" Thomas replied. "You're now a scavenger. It's our job to clear the cotton fibres around the spinning machines."

"You want me to crawl under the machines?" EJ gulped. "That looks dangerous."

"I've witnessed my fair share of accidents," said Thomas.

As the spinning frames rotated, the bobbins began to fill with spun cotton thread. Aniyah cradled empty bobbins in her arms and tried to anticipate which one would be full first.

"Mr Elliot's in a foul mood today," Aniyah overheard a woman say.

It was Barbara. She was working alongside Susan. They were watching the machines closely and controlling the speed and tension.

"I hear there's been a lot of unrest. Some of the workers are refusing to touch the raw cotton," explained Barbara.

"Over wages?" Susan asked.

Barbara shook her head. "No, there's this lady from the United States. She's been going around the country giving speeches. She says the raw cotton is picked by enslaved people who are treated poorly."

Aniyah moved in closer.

"Oh, now that you mention it, there was something in the paper. Her name's Sarah Parker Remond. Do you think she'll come here?" Susan asked.

"Well, that's just it," Barbara said. "She's been in Scotland giving speeches, and she's here in Manchester to give a talk at the Athenaeum today!"

Manchester ... that's it, we're in Manchester in 1859! thought Aniyah.

"That bobbin over there," Annie shouted over the noise. "It's full. Swap it over, quick!"

Aniyah dodged through the workers and stretched out her doffer hook, just like Annie had shown her. The full bobbin came out of the spinning frame.

Suddenly a loud scream pierced the air.

"What's going on?" asked Barbara.

"I think it's one of the new scavengers," someone called over.

Aniyah dropped her doffer hook. "EJ!"

Chapter 4

Aniyah weaved around the other workers.

Olivia had heard the noise, too. "I think it was EJ!"

"It sounded like he was hurt!" Aniyah replied.

They found Mr Elliot standing over EJ, yelling. "Get under there and clean the machines!"

"I can't!" EJ spluttered. "It's too difficult. That thing almost took my head off!"

"It's not the only thing that'll have your head!" Mr Elliot raised his hand in the air.

Aniyah lifted her foot and kicked over a pile of large threads. They hit Mr Elliot.

Thomas grinned. "I'd run for it if I were you."

"*Ruuun!*" yelled EJ. He jumped up and headed for the exit. Aniyah and Olivia sprinted after him.

They charged through the doors of Ancoat's Cotton & Co and back onto the street. Mr Elliot's angry yells chased after them like bloodthirsty hounds.

"Freedom!" yelled EJ. "It was like a prison in there."

"What do we do now?" asked Olivia.

"I need something to eat," said EJ.

"We have no money," said Aniyah.

Just then, Aniyah noticed a woman flag down a hansom cab.

"To the Athenaeum," the woman requested.

She held her hat in place while she climbed in. An envelope flew from her coat pocket.

"Wait, you dropped something!" cried Aniyah, but the cab had already pulled away.

EJ picked up the envelope; the seal was broken, and the contents poked out.

“What is it?” asked Olivia.

EJ prised the letter out. “It’s just gibberish,” he said.

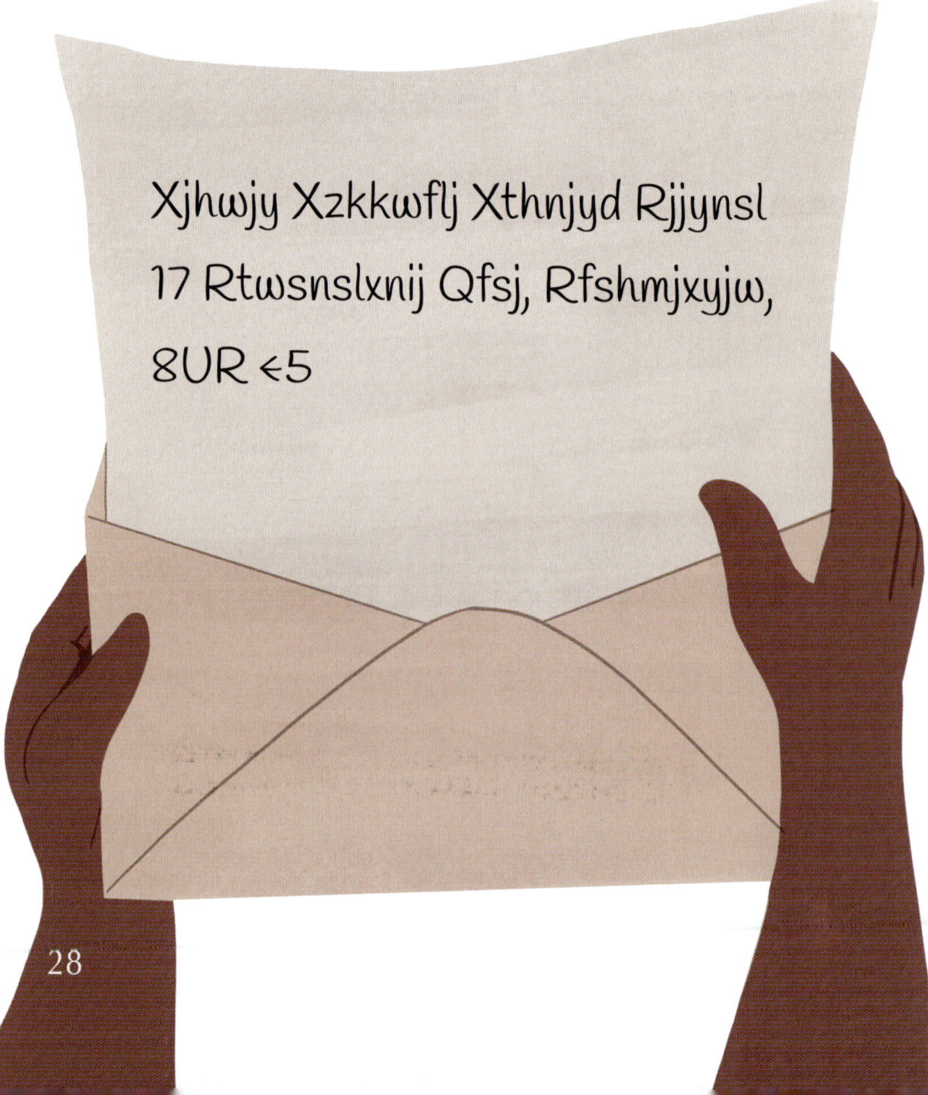

"There's a name on the envelope – Sarah Parker Remond," Olivia said.

"The women in the mill were talking about her," Aniyah replied. "We're in Manchester, and she's giving a talk on the rights of enslaved people at the Athenaeum."

"But how are we going to find the Athenaeum?" Olivia asked.

"I have just the thing," said EJ, unfurling the map.

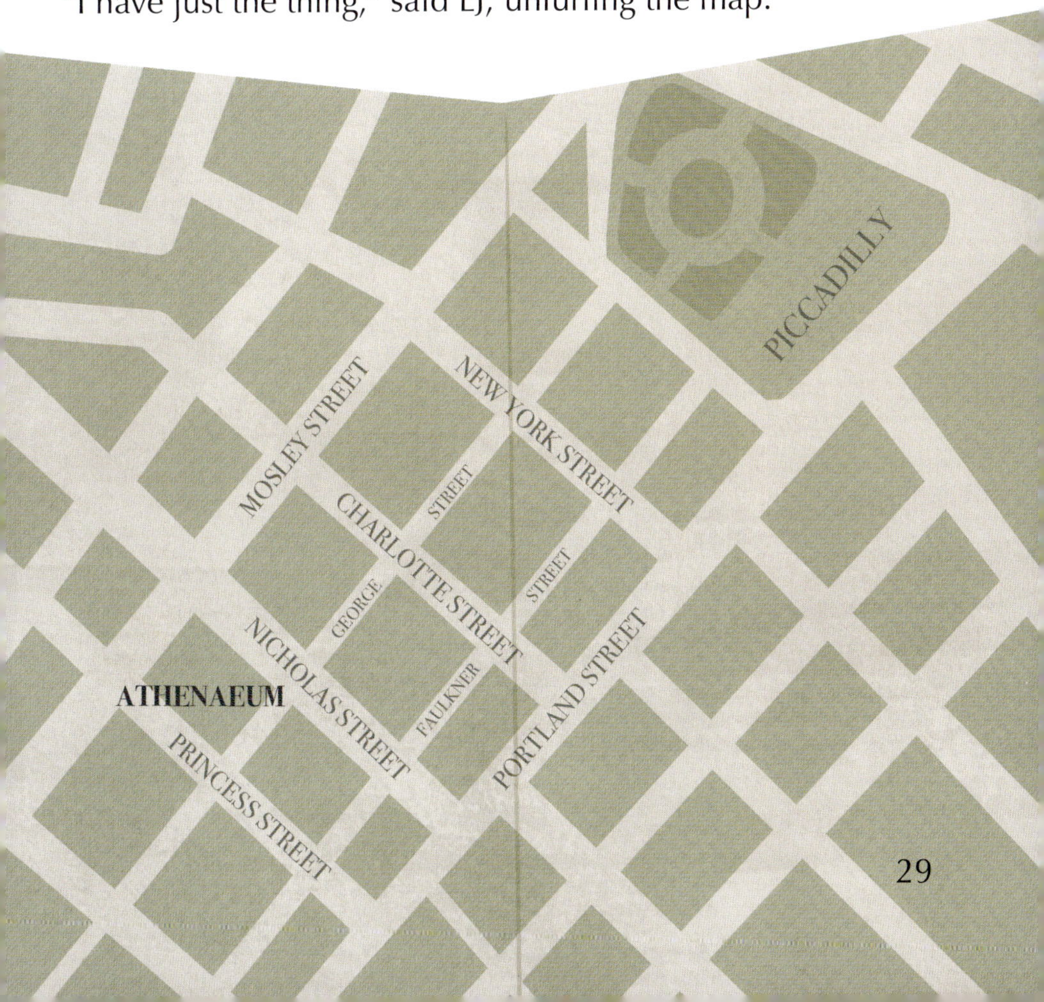

The Athenaeum stood proud, its many windows beckoned outsiders to imagine the stories and artefacts behind its panes.

Inside, it had high ceilings, elegant chandeliers and rows of bookshelves. The smell of aged paper and leather bindings lingered in the air. The stained-glass windows cast a kaleidoscope of colours onto the marble floor.

They walked through a gallery and into a small hall.

"There's the woman who dropped the letter," said Aniyah. "I think the talk's about to begin."

"Good evening. I am Sarah Parker Remond; I'm a lecturer, activist and abolitionist."

"What's an abolitionist?" whispered EJ.

"An abolitionist is against the practice of enslavement and seeks to end it." Sarah's voice echoed around the hall as though in direct response.

“For the enslaved, there is no home, no hope, no help. When I walk through the streets of Manchester and see its cotton mills, I think of the enslaved people who work on the 80,000 cotton plantations where cotton is grown for your market,” explained Sarah.

After her speech, everyone stood and clapped.

Sarah started handing out flyers.

"Your speech was inspiring!" Aniyah told her.

"Thank you kindly," Sarah replied. "I gave my first public speech when I was 16 years old. I've delivered abolitionist speeches across the United States, and now I'm here to gain support for the cause."

"Although I was born a freewoman, and my parents were successful business owners, I faced discrimination," Sarah continued. "As a child I was expelled from school because of the colour of my skin. It's injustices like these that give me the fuel to fight."

“We’ll hand out the flyers,” EJ offered.

“That would be swell!” said Sarah, handing them each a pile. “I must be going shortly; I have another important meeting.”

She rummaged through her pockets and her face fell. “Oh no! It’s gone!”

Chapter 5

EJ reached into his pocket. "Are you looking for this?"

Sarah looked at him in amazement. "Why, yes!"

"You dropped it earlier; we came here to find you," Aniyah said.

"We looked at the letter, but we couldn't understand it," Olivia confessed.

"Can you keep a secret?" asked Sarah.

Aniyah, Olivia and EJ nodded.

"Some people don't like change. I attend lots of important meetings with like-minded people who want to see things change for enslaved people. We use a Caesar cipher in case our letters end up in the wrong hands."

"The hands of the people who don't want things to change?" asked Aniyah.

"Exactly!" said Sarah.

"What's a Caesar cipher?" asked EJ.

"It's a way of encrypting a message using a code," Sarah replied. "Each letter is swapped with another letter so no one can read the original message."

"How can *you* read the original message, then?" Olivia asked.

"You need a key. Once you have the key, you can decode the message." Sarah pointed to the letter. "You see this number five after the arrow? This tells me to shift the letters backwards by five. Take the first letter, 'x'. If you count back five letters, you get 's'."

"We can help with that!" EJ said.

"Sure, use my pencil," Sarah replied.

Olivia wrote out the alphabet on the back of a flyer and they got to work.

Letters in the message

A	B	C	D	E	F	G	H	I	J	K	L	M
V	W	X	Y	Z	A	B	C	D	E	F	G	H

N	O	P	Q	R	S	T	U	V	W	X	Y	Z
I	J	K	L	M	N	O	P	Q	R	S	T	U

Shift back by five (<5)

Secret

Xjhwjy Xzkkwflj Xthnjyd Rjjynsl

17 Rtwsnslxnij Qfsj, Rfshmjxyjw,

8UR <5

"We've decoded the message!" Olivia said, proudly.

Secret Suffrage Society Meeting

Xjhwjy Xzkkwflj Xthnjyd Rjjynsl

17 Morningside Lane, Manchester

17 Rtwsnslxnij Qfsj, Rfshmjxyjw,

8PM

8UR <5

Sarah looked down at the letter. “I don’t suppose you know where Morningside Lane is?”

“Not exactly, but we do have something that might help.” EJ handed the map to Sarah.

“Thank you!” Sarah reached into her bag and offered them some coins.

"What now?" asked Olivia, once Sarah had disappeared down the street.

EJ jingled the coins. "Now, we finally get something to eat!" he smiled.

Suddenly a tornado that formed a wormhole pulled them in.

Chapter 6

"I didn't like having a real job," said EJ. "Working in that cotton mill was hard work."

"Those kids we met were really young. We're lucky we can go to school, and have time to play," Olivia said.

"I hope Mr Elliot gets swallowed up by a weaving loom!" Aniyah replied.

“Should we play again?” asked Olivia. “My fingers hurt from tying the thread.”

“What I really need right now is rest,” said Aniyah. “My arms still ache from changing those bobbins.”

EJ collapsed onto the old sofa. “World domination will have to wait!”

Make your own Caesar cipher

1. Write out the alphabet

A	B	C	D	E	F	G	H	I	J	K	L	M	N	O	P	Q	R	S	T	U	V	W	X	Y	Z

2. Choose a number to shift the letters backwards, or forwards

3. If you choose to shift the letters backwards by five, for example, the key will be <5

4. If you choose to shift the letters forwards by five, the key will be >5

5. Write out a second alphabet, under the first one, with the letters shifted. This shows the letters shifted back by 5 (<5)

A	B	C	D	E	F	G	H	I	J	K	L	M	N	O	P	Q	R	S	T	U	V	W	X	Y	Z
V	W	X	Y	Z	A	B	C	D	E	F	G	H	I	J	K	L	M	N	O	P	Q	R	S	T	U

6. Write your coded message, and put the key at the end

7. Give the coded message to a friend and ask them to work out what you've written.

REAL PEOPLE

Sarah Parker Remond

1826–1894

Sarah Parker Remond was an African-American abolitionist. She began campaigning when she was 16 and travelled across the US and to Europe to speak against the practice.

Sarah did visit the Manchester Athenaeum in 1859 and was greeted by enthusiastic crowds who shared her views.

Ideas for reading

Written by Gill Matthews
Primary Literacy Consultant

Reading objectives:

- check that the text makes sense to them, discuss their understanding, and explaining the meaning of words in context
- draw inferences such as inferring characters' feelings, thoughts and motives from their actions, and justifying inferences with evidence
- participate in discussion about both books that are read to them and those they can read for themselves, taking turns and listening to what others say

Spoken language objectives:

- use relevant strategies to build their vocabulary
- articulate and justify answers, arguments and opinions
- use spoken language to develop understanding through speculating, hypothesising, imagining and exploring ideas

Curriculum links: Relationships education: Respectful relationships

Interest words: cramped, weathered, cobblestone, etched, jostled, unison

Build a context for reading

- Ask children to look at the front cover of the book and to describe what they can see.
- Discuss what they think a *cipher* might be.
- Read the back-cover blurb and encourage children to talk about what they think the book is about.

Understand and apply reading strategies

- Read pp2–4 aloud, demonstrating how to use meaning, punctuation and dialogue to help you to read with appropriate expression.
- Ask children when and where they think the story is set. Encourage them to support their responses with reasons and evidence from the text.
- Children can read pp5–12, using the strategies that you demonstrated to help them read with expression.
- Discuss where and when the children think EJ, Olivia and Aniyah have been transported to.